CLASSIC
StoryTellers

ERNEST HEMINGWAY

Mitchell Lane
PUBLISHERS

P.O. Box 196
Hockessin, Delaware 19707

Titles in the Series

Beverly Cleary

E. B. White

Edgar Allan Poe

Ernest Hemingway

F. Scott Fitzgerald

Harriet Beecher Stowe

Jack London

Jacqueline Woodson

John Steinbeck

Judy Blume

Katherine Paterson

Mark Twain

Matt Christopher

Mildred Taylor

Nathaniel Hawthorne

Ray Bradbury

Stephen Crane

CLASSIC
StoryTellers

ERNEST HEMINGWAY

Jim Whiting

Printing   2   3   4   5   6   7   8

          Library of Congress Cataloging-in-Publication Data
Whiting, Jim, 1943-
          Ernest Hemingway / by Jim Whiting.
                    p. cm — (Classic storytellers)
          Includes bibliographical references and index.
          ISBN 1-58415-376-8 (library bound)
1. Hemingway, Ernest, 1899-1961—Juvenile literature. 2. Authors, American—20th century Biography—Juvenile literature. I. Title. II. Series.
PS3515.E37Z9475 2005
813'.52—dc22   2004030261

ISBN 13: 9781584153764

J-B
HEMINGWAY
381-0499

ABOUT THE AUTHOR: Jim Whiting has been a journalist, writer, editor, and photographer for more than 20 years. In addition to a lengthy stint as publisher of *Northwest Runner* magazine, Mr. Whiting has contributed articles to the *Seattle Times, Conde Nast Traveler, Newsday,* and *Saturday Evening Post.* He has written and edited more than 160 Mitchell Lane titles. He lives in Washington state with his wife and two teenage sons.

PHOTO CREDITS: Cover, pp. 1, 3, 6 Getty Images; pp. 14, 19, 22 John Fitzgerald Kennedy Library; pp. 30, 36 Getty Images; p. 39 Library of Congress

PUBLISHER'S NOTE: This story is based on the author's extensive research, which he believes to be accurate. Documentation of such research is contained on pages 46-47.

The internet sites referenced herein were active as of the publication date. Due to the fleeting nature of some web sites, we cannot guarantee they will all be active when you are reading this book.

PLB2,4

Contents

ERNEST HEMINGWAY
Jim Whiting

Chapter 1   The Ones That Didn't Get Away ... 7
*FYInfo: Other American Nobel
Prize for Literature Winners 13

Chapter 2   A Midwest Boy Goes to War 15
FYInfo: The Spanish-American
War 21

Chapter 3   Breaking In with a Bang 23
FYInfo: Bullfighting 29

Chapter 4   Creating the Legend 31
FYInfo: F. Scott Fitzgerald 35

Chapter 5   The Final Triumph 37
FYInfo: Fidel Castro and
the Cuban Revolution 42

Chronology 43
Selected Works 43
Timeline in History 44
Chapter Notes 45
Further Reading 46-47
    For Young Adults 46
    Works Consulted 46
    On the Internet 46-47
Glossary   47
Index 48

*For Your Information

StoryTellers StoryTellers StoryTellers StoryTellers StoryTellers StoryTellers StoryTellers

From a very young age, Ernest Hemingway loved to fish. He is pictured here holding two trout that he caught in 1939 on the Wood River near Sun Valley, Idaho. By this time he had established a reputation as one of this country's most important authors.

Chapter 1

THE ONES THAT
DIDN'T GET AWAY

Fishermen love to talk about the fish they catch. They love even more to talk about "the one that got away." They brag about how big it was. Sometimes it seems as if the mysterious fish gets bigger every time the story is told. It doesn't matter. Everyone enjoys listening.

From a very young age, Ernest Hemingway loved to fish. Many of the pictures taken of him during his life show him proudly holding fish he had hooked. In the beginning, they were small. Some were only a few inches long. When he became an adult, he often went deep-sea fishing. There the fish were much bigger. Some weighed hundreds of pounds and were several feet long.

Two of Hemingway's most famous stories are about fishing. One is "The Big Two-Hearted River," a short story he wrote in the early 1920s. Nearly three decades later, he wrote the short novel *The Old Man and the Sea*. In each of these stories, the fish doesn't get away. To realize why we consider Hemingway to be a classic storyteller, it is important to understand some of the reasons why the fish were caught.

"The Big Two-Hearted River" begins when a young war veteran named Nick Adams gets off the train near a town in upper Michigan he had visited several years earlier. To his surprise, the town has burned to the ground. No one lives there anymore. Carrying a heavy backpack, he takes off on a long hike to the Big Two-Hearted River. When he finds a good campsite, he pitches his tent, has dinner, then settles in for the night. He gets up early the next morning and goes fishing. He catches two fish, cleans them, and heads back to his camp.

It appears to be a very simple story. Many people finish reading it and wonder what it was about. Nothing seems to happen.

But it is very important that "nothing happens." Nick has recently returned from fighting in World War I. He was wounded in combat. More important is what the war did to his mind. When Hemingway wrote the story, no one had heard of post-traumatic stress disorder. This condition is one from which thousands of Vietnam veterans and those who fought in Iraq suffer. In Hemingway's era, it was known more simply as "shell shock" or "combat fatigue." No matter what the condition is called, it is a reflection of the way that people may react to the pressures of combat. They are shot at, they listen to sporadic explosions, and they live under the constant threat of being seriously wounded or killed.

Post-traumatic means "after a potentially harmful event." In the story, Nick is still afraid even though he is no longer in a combat situation. He is safely back in the United States, but the memories of the horrible things he witnessed continue to haunt him. Nick goes fishing because it is one of his favorite ways of relaxing. Even more important, it is something he has done so many times that he has developed a set of habits. Hemingway spends a lot of time describing routine things such as pitching the tent, fixing coffee, and gathering grasshoppers. Nick focuses his attention on these simple things because it keeps his mind from wandering into areas that he is afraid of.

Hemingway uses the landscape to show Nick's feelings. The scorched earth where the town used to stand is a reflection of the death and destruction that Nick experienced during the fighting. He has to get away from it as soon as possible. The paths he follows, the woods in which he camps, the river itself are all unspoiled and comforting.

But not everything in nature offers comfort. There is a swamp not far from his campsite. The swamp represents danger. Nick needs to stay out in the open and away from the swamp until he feels better.

"The river became smooth and deep and the swamp looked solid with cedar trees, their trunks close together, their branches solid," Hemingway writes. "It would not be possible to walk through a swamp like that. . . . In the swamp fishing was a tragic adventure."[1]

Many readers might expect that a horrible monster is lurking in the swamp. At some point, when Nick is feeling relaxed, the monster might come out and attack him. Perhaps the story would end with Nick's blood flowing down the river.

There is no monster. There is no attack. There is no blood flowing down the river. Nick spends a peaceful day fishing. He skillfully catches two large trout. After he cleans them, he gets ready to go back to his camp, where he will eat the two fish for his dinner. The story concludes, "There were plenty of days coming when he could fish the swamp."[2]

That is an optimistic ending. Nick will stay in his camp and will overcome his problem. Someday he will probe the dangers of the swamp. Not just yet.

In the mid-1930s, when Hemingway was a successful and famous author, he liked to spend time in Cuba. He bought a fishing boat and hired a man named Carlos Gutiérrez to serve as the boat's captain. He spent many days far offshore, happily fishing for marlin. Marlin are huge fish with a short, pointed snout.

One day, Gutiérrez told Hemingway a story. The story made a deep impression on the writer, and he retold it soon afterward in a magazine article. "An old man fishing alone in a skiff out of Cabañas hooked a great marlin that, on the heavy sashcord handline, pulled the skiff out to the sea," Hemingway wrote. "Two days later the old man was picked up by fishermen sixty miles to the eastward . . ."[3] (Cabañas is a small fishing village on the northern coast of Cuba.)

Hemingway thought about the story for a long time. As Gutiérrez explained it to him, the fisherman's ordeal had almost driven him crazy. But one thing about being a writer is that Hemingway could invent his own ending. That is exactly what he did when he wrote *The Old Man and the Sea* years later. His hero is a down-on-his-luck Cuban fisherman named Santiago.

Hemingway begins the story by saying, "He was an old man who fished alone in a skiff in the Gulf Stream and he had gone eighty-four days now without taking a fish."[4]

For the people in his fishing village, the long weeks of failure are a bad sign. The boy who once crewed for him has long since been forbidden to accompany him anymore. The boy goes out with other men who don't have any trouble catching fish. Even Santiago's boat reflects his desperate condition: "The sail was patched with flour sacks and, furled, it looked like the flag of permanent defeat."[5]

But Santiago, like the heroes of Hemingway's other stories, does not accept defeat. "Man is not made for defeat," Hemingway writes. "A man can be destroyed but not defeated."[6]

Hemingway biographer Jeffrey Meyers notes, "Like the hero of 'Big Two-Hearted River,' Santiago engages in the ritual of fishing and tests his inner strength while isolated in the natural element."[7]

While Santiago is not suffering from shell shock, he is just as careful as Nick to observe his fishing rituals. Finally his luck seems to turn. He hooks a huge marlin, which drags him far out of sight of land. When the fish surfaces and Santiago sees him for the first time, he is awestruck.

"The line rose slowly and steadily and then the surface of the ocean bulged ahead of the boat and the fish came out. He came out unendingly and water poured from his sides . . . ," Hemingway wrote. "Now alone, and out of sight of land, [Santiago] was fast to the biggest fish that he had ever seen and bigger than he had ever heard of . . ."[8]

The story certainly hooked its readers. Even though it is considered to be a novel, it was short enough to be published in a single issue of *Life* magazine, one of the most popular publications of that era. It sold 5 million copies in just over 48 hours. When it was released in book form, it continued to do well. It was a selection of the Book of the Month Club.

The Old Man and the Sea also hooked the critics. In 1953, the book won the Pulitzer Prize, probably the most prestigious award for writing in the United States. It would go on to net an even bigger award: the Nobel Prize for Literature in 1954. Even though

Hemingway was one of the world's most famous writers, he had never before been considered for the Nobel Prize.

". . . Hemingway's earlier writings display brutal, cynical, and callous sides which may be considered at variance with the Nobel Prize's requirement for a work of an ideal tendency,"[9] said Anders Österling, Permanent Secretary of the Swedish Academy, during his presentation speech at the award ceremony.

The Old Man and the Sea erased those objections. "[C]ourage is Hemingway's central theme—the bearing of one who is put to the test and who steels himself to meet the cold cruelty of existence . . . ," Österling continued. He also said, "Within the frame of a sporting tale, a moving perspective of man's destiny is opened up; the story is a tribute to the fighting spirit, which does not give in."[10]

Österling's feelings were shared by many other people who considered the award as the high point of Hemingway's career. Unfortunately, Hemingway apparently lost his own fighting spirit within a few years. His life, which had so many triumphs, was destined to end in tragedy.

FYInfo

Other American Nobel Prize for Literature Winners

1930: Sinclair Lewis (1885–1951).
Born in Minnesota, Lewis wrote five novels that attracted little attention before *Main Street*, published in 1920, established his reputation. He followed that with *Babbitt* (1922), *Arrowsmith* (1925), *Elmer Gantry* (1927), *Dodsworth* (1929), and many others.

1936: Eugene O'Neill (1888–1953).
The son of an actor, O'Neill wrote more than a dozen highly regarded plays in the 1920s and early 1930s. His most famous work, *Long Day's Journey into Night*, was produced following his death.

1938: Pearl Buck (1892–1973).
Born in West Virginia, Buck spent much of her early life in China, where her parents were missionaries. This experience led to *The Good Earth* (1931), her most famous work.

1949: William Faulkner (1897–1962). The country's most famous southern novelist, Faulkner wrote about racial conflict and the decline of the Old South in such novels as *The Sound and the Fury* (1929), *Sanctuary* (1931), and *Light in August* (1932). He was also a Hollywood screenwriter.

1962: John Steinbeck (1902–1968). Steinbeck is most famous for *The Grapes of Wrath* (1939), a novel about a migrant family looking for work in California during the Great Depression. Most of his other books also explore social issues.

1976: Saul Bellow (1915–2005).
Born in Canada, Bellow moved perma-

Joseph Brodsky

nently to the United States when he was nine. His novels, which include *Herzog* (1964), *Mr. Sammler's Planet* (1970), and *Humboldt's Gift* (1975), have won major national and international awards. He also wrote plays and essays.

1978: Isaac Bashevis Singer (1904–1991). Born in Poland, Singer became a U.S. citizen in 1943. In addition to novels and short stories, he wrote memoirs and children's books. Many of his stories describe Jewish life in the early 1900s.

1987: Joseph Brodsky (1940–1996). Brodsky was born in the Soviet Union (now Russia). Soviet officials did not like his poetry and essays. Brodsky came to the United States and became a citizen in 1980.

1993: Toni Morrison (1931–).
Morrison's novels, such as *The Bluest Eye* (1970), *Song of Solomon* (1977), *Tar Baby* (1981), and *Beloved* (1987), depict African American life. She is also an editor, a book critic, and a university professor.

Ernest Hemingway stands at the right in this family photo, which was probably taken when he was seven. His father Clarence holds Carol, while Madelaine (Sunny) sits on his mother Grace's lap. His older sister Marcelline is at the left of the picture.

Chapter 2

A MIDWEST BOY
GOES TO WAR

When she was young, Grace Hall suffered a severe case of scarlet fever that permanently weakened her eyes—but she had a beautiful voice. She dreamed of becoming an opera singer. When she was old enough, she moved to New York City, hoping she could start her career there. She was very disappointed to find that the lights on an operatic stage were too strong for her eyesight. She moved back to Oak Park, Illinois, where she had grown up, and began giving singing lessons. Soon afterward, she married Clarence Hemingway, whom she had known in high school.

On July 21, 1899, Grace gave birth to Ernest Miller Hemingway. Clarence Hemingway, the boy's father, was the doctor who delivered him.

Ernest joined a sister, Marcelline, who was a year and a half older. In 1902, his sister Ursula was born. Two years later, Madelaine (whose nickname was Sunny) joined the family. Yet another sister, Carol, was born in 1911. The family was completed with the birth of their kid brother, Leicester (pronounced LES-tur), in 1915.

Because Ernest and Marcelline were relatively close in age, their mother often referred to them as twins. She even dressed them alike when they were young, usually in girls' clothing.

The family spent much of every summer at their cabin by Walloon Lake, near the northeast corner of Lake Michigan. Those summers marked the beginning of Ernest's lifelong love for fishing—he caught his first fish when he was only three—and other forms of outdoor recreation. He learned how to camp and to hunt birds and small game. His experiences at the lake provided him with plenty of material for some of his most memorable short stories.

Both of Ernest's grandfathers fought in the Civil War. The impressionable boy grew up with their stories of military heroism, which greatly influenced him. The title of one of his books, *Across the River and Into the Trees,* is derived from the final words of the dying Confederate general Stonewall Jackson.

His grandfathers weren't his only military influence. The Spanish-American War had taken place the year before his birth. The United States was still proud of its swift victory. Thousands of miles away, the Boer War and the Russo-Japanese War received a great deal of publicity during the boy's early years. Ernest also liked the Old Testament of the Bible because of all the battles.

His parents, especially his mother, approved of his reading the Bible. Like most of the residents of Oak Park, the family was very religious. His sister Sunny later wrote, "We always said the blessing before meals. We had morning family prayers, accompanied by a Bible reading and the singing of a hymn or two. Our family was expected to go to church each Sunday."[1]

The emphasis on prayer didn't keep Ernest from pretending that he was a great hunter or a courageous soldier. At the age of five, he boasted that he grabbed a galloping horse and quickly pulled it to a halt. His mother later recalled that he didn't seem afraid of anything. This fearlessness had a downside. It was fortunate that his father was a doctor because Ernest often hurt himself. One of the worse injuries occurred when he fell while running at full speed with a stick in his mouth. The stick seriously gouged his throat. Incidents such as these would plague him for his entire life. Biographer Jeffrey Meyers takes three pages to list all the accidents, illnesses, and other health problems that continued up until Hemingway's death.[2] Many of these were due to the seeming need to prove his courage that had begun while he was still very young and continued all his life.

He also had one specific medical condition. From a very early age, he had difficulties seeing out of his left eye. At first he blamed his mother because of her own defective vision. In later life—trying to consciously cut himself free from her influence—he shifted the blame to sneaky boxing opponents.

His vision problem didn't keep him from developing an early love for reading. It was his favorite thing to do when he started school, and it probably contributed to the talent for writing that he showed in 1911. "His teacher at Holmes Grammar School praised him for a story called 'My First Sea Voyage,'" writes biographer Richard B. Lyttle. "Although Ernest did not admit it in school, the story was based almost entirely on his uncle Tyley Hancock's childhood experience. In adopting someone else's experience as his own, Ernest had learned a basic tool of the storyteller's art."[3]

Ernest entered Oak Park and River Forest Township High School in September 1913. He tried out for football, but the coach told him that at five feet, four inches, he was too small. By his junior year, he was finally big enough to play football. He joined the swimming and water polo teams, and also learned to box. He became somewhat of a bully, as he had grown larger than most of the people he knew.

His writing ability had also developed. His English teachers often read his compositions aloud to the other students in their classes, and he wrote regularly for the school newspaper. Even though many of his classmates were thinking about going on to college, Ernest showed very little interest. One reason was that he was eager to leave home. He was getting into trouble with his family. Another was that, by the time he graduated in 1917, the United States had entered World War I. Ernest talked about joining the army, but his father refused to grant permission. Instead, he had one of Ernest's uncles find a job for Ernest in Kansas City, Missouri. He would become a reporter with the *Kansas City Star.* Ernest looked forward to the change.

It didn't take him long to settle into life in Kansas City. Hemingway enjoyed his newspaper job. The older reporters liked the enthusiastic young man. They taught him how to write short, clearly phrased sentences that avoided the use of adjectives. This lesson would come in valuable a few years later when he applied this technique to writing fiction.

By the end of 1917, it was apparent that some of his friends on the paper would be called up for military service. The war seemed like an adventure, and Hemingway wanted to be a part of it. He knew that his bad eyesight would keep him from joining the army, but it wouldn't keep him from driving an ambulance. He applied to the Red Cross and was accepted. In May 1918, he went to New York. Soon he was on a ship heading for Europe.

When he returned from World War I, Hemingway liked to wear uniforms like this one. He hadn't been a soldier. But he wanted to look like one.

Hemingway wanted to serve in France. Instead, the Red Cross sent him to Milan, Italy, where he learned how to drive the big ambulances. Then he went to a field hospital in the mountains. Even though he was only a few miles from the front lines, there was almost no danger. Bored, he asked for a transfer so that he could be even closer to the action. He was sent to the village of Fossalta, which was north of Venice and near the Piave River. The Italians were on the south side of the river; the Austrians occupied the northern bank. Hemingway enjoyed riding his bike to the front lines. He took cigarettes and other treats to the men in the trenches. They were happy to see him, and they taught him how to speak Italian.

The evening of July 8 was warm. There was little gunfire as Hemingway parked his bike and crept up to the edge of the river. Soon the fighting flared up. The opposing forces were trading increasing amounts of mortar and machine-gun fire across the river. Hemingway was about to gain firsthand experience of the horrors of war.

FYInfo

World War I in Italy

After more than two and a half years of neutrality in World War I, the United States had declared war on Germany in April, 1917. Thousands of American troops had begun arriving there soon afterward. Almost all the newspaper stories in the United States were about their "boys" in France, where they joined English and French troops. It was natural for Ernest to want to help his countrymen when he arrived in Europe.

Benito Mussolini

Even though Italy had signed the Triple Alliance with Germany and Austria-Hungary in 1882, the country remained neutral when the war began in August, 1914. Both of the opposing sides tried to persuade the Italians to enter the war on their side. After secret negotiations with England and France, Italy declared war on Austria-Hungary in May, 1915.

One reason was to obtain several small regions that Italy considered part of its natural territory but which lay under the domination of Austria-Hungary. Another was the serious decline in the economy. Traditional markets in France and Germany were closed, while imports of raw materials had substantially decreased. Italian leaders believed that war would give a major boost to business.

As was the case in France, the war had settled down to an exhaustive, inconclusive series of battles that did little else except kill and wound tens of thousands of troops. That changed late in 1917. The Austria-Hungarians achieved almost complete surprise at the battle of Caporetto. They killed or captured tens of thousands of Italians and pushed them back to the Piave River, where the attack stalled. Each dug in on its side of the river. That was still the situation when Ernest arrived several months later.

After the fighting ended in November, 1918, Italy gained most of the territory that it had desired from the defeated Austria-Hungarians. But the so-called "victory" had created severe economic problems in Italy. These problems laid the foundation for the rise of Benito Mussolini, who became the country's dictator in 1926 and led Italy into World War II on the side of Nazi Germany.

No 359666

This is Ernest Hemingway's passport photo. It was taken around 1923, when he and his wife Hadley moved to Paris. He soon met several people who helped him in his writing career.

Chapter 3

BREAKING IN WITH A BANG

There was nothing fancy or sophisticated about the shells that were being fired in Hemingway's direction. They were simply cans filled with gunpowder and pieces of razor-sharp scrap metal. One of these shells exploded a few feet from Hemingway. The blast knocked him down. More than 200 tiny metal fragments sliced into him. A man who had been standing a few feet away was killed instantly. Another was badly wounded. Hemingway picked up the wounded man and began carrying him toward safety. Austrian machine gunners across the river opened fire. A few bullets smashed into Hemingway's legs. Somehow he covered the remaining distance to the first aid station, still carrying the wounded man. Then he passed out.

For his heroism, he was awarded the Italian Silver Cross of Merit. He was taken to the hospital where he had originally arrived a few weeks earlier. During his recovery, he fell in love with one of the nurses, Agnes von Kurowsky. She was attracted to him as well, but there was one problem. She was nearly thirty and

Hemingway was still a teenager. The age difference didn't seem to matter to him. When they were separated after Agnes went to a hospital in Florence, Italy, he thought that they would be together again.

He was still in love with Agnes early in 1919 when he returned to Oak Park, where he was considered a hero. He looked very dashing in his uniform and an Italian cloak. He wrote passionate letters to Agnes, but she had fallen in love with another man. Eventually Grace Hemingway got tired of her son hanging around the house and doing nothing all day. Ernest moved to Chicago, where he shared an apartment with a friend. He sent articles to a Canadian newspaper, the *Toronto Star,* and tried to have his short stories published.

In the fall of 1920, he met a woman named Elizabeth Hadley Richardson at a party. Even though she was eight years older than Hemingway, they fell in love. They were married in 1921. Ernest still wasn't making much money, but Hadley (as everyone called her) had a trust fund. The annual income was enough for them to live on. Soon they decided to go to Europe, which Ernest thought would be a better place to pursue his ambition to become a writer. Hadley supported the decision. At first they wanted to go to Italy, but Sherwood Anderson, a famous writer, told them to go to Paris instead. He said that there were many writers there. It helped that the Toronto *Star* agreed to pay Hemingway to write a series of articles, which he called *Letters from Europe*. Anderson also gave him some letters of introduction to several people in Paris who might be able to help his career.

One of these people was Gertrude Stein, an art collector and writer who had lived in Paris for many years. She gave Hemingway advice about his writing. He also met Ezra Pound, a well-known poet. Pound helped him with the style he had already begun to develop with the *Kansas City Star:* short sentences and clear, precise images. In return, Hemingway gave Pound boxing lessons.

The Hemingways settled into a cheap apartment in Paris. They had enough money to afford something better but chose to spend their money on experiences such as skiing vacations. Ernest and Hadley had a lot of fun, but they never lost sight of the main reason for being in Paris: to advance Ernest's career. He spent much of his time writing. Once Ernest left Paris to go on a trip by himself. A few days later, Hadley joined him. He had asked her to bring a suitcase that contained nearly all of his stories. She set it down on a train platform and walked a short distance away. When she returned, she found to her horror that someone had stolen it. Ernest was furious. Eventually, he got over his anger.

In 1923 Hemingway began to experience success. Anderson had already helped him by getting a few lines of his poetry printed in a literary journal that was based in New Orleans. Now Hemingway published *Three Stories & Ten Poems*. Only 300 copies were printed, but several reviewers commented favorably. Later that year he and Hadley—who was pregnant and wanted a diversion—vacationed in Spain. Ernest discovered bullfighting, which would become a lifelong passion. While he could never become a professional matador and confront a dangerous bull face to face in the bullring, the sport did offer him a chance to prove his courage. According to a longstanding tradition in Pamplona, a city in northern Spain, the bulls that would be used in afternoon bullfights were released from their pens in the morning about half a mile from the bullring. The bulls would run through the streets, and dozens of people would run in front of them. It was risky, because the bulls were faster and weighed several times as much as the people. Being gored by a bull's horn was very painful. Sometimes it resulted in death. Hemingway loved "the running of the bulls." It was thrilling for him to dash up the street with the huge animals only a few feet away. Once the bulls had arrived in the ring, they provided another way of facing danger. Their horns would be thickly padded, and people could come down in the ring and face them, waving coats or shirts in front of them. While the padding prevented anyone from being gored, the object was to get close to the bulls without actually making contact. Finally, the bullfighting would begin. Hemingway particularly admired a matador named Nicanor.

The Hemingways moved from France to Toronto, Canada, believing that Hadley would receive better medical care there than in Paris. Hemingway took a newspaper job, which he hated. In October 1923, John Hadley Nicanor Hemingway was born.

Within three months the family was back in Paris. With Anderson's help, *In Our Time,* a collection of Hemingway's short stories, was published. Many of the stories, such as "The Big Two-Hearted River," are based on Hemingway's own experiences.

The following year he got his first big break. Another American writer living in Paris, F. Scott Fitzgerald, read some of Hemingway's stories. Fitzgerald was already famous for his novels *This Side of Paradise* and *The Beautiful and the Damned.* He recommended Hemingway to Maxwell Perkins, his editor at Charles Scribner's Sons, a major New York publisher. Perkins is considered one of the greatest editors in American publishing history. He took a gamble on Hemingway, who was almost unknown in the United States. He offered him an advance—money paid to an author before a book is published—for a novel he was working on.

Perkins's gamble paid off. Published in 1926, *The Sun Also Rises* created a sensation. Based on his experiences traveling around Europe with a group of friends, it introduced Hemingway's style to countless numbers of readers. Critics praised it as an accurate depiction of the "lost generation," young people whose idealism and illusions had been smashed during the more than four years of seemingly senseless slaughter of World War I. The book immediately marked the twenty-seven-year-old author as one of the country's finest young novelists.

It also marked a division between Ernest and Hadley. Not long before, he had met Pauline Pfeiffer, a magazine editor, and he wanted to marry her. He asked Hadley for a divorce, but he felt guilty about abandoning her. He arranged for her to receive all the royalties from *The Sun Also Rises.*

His divorce may not have been the only upheaval in his life. Professional critics may have loved *The Sun Also Rises,* but one amateur critic did not. One day he got a letter that said his book was "one of the filthiest books of the year."[1] The critic was his mother. When the book group of which she was a member decided to read it, she walked out.

In 1927, Hemingway married Pauline. When she became pregnant, they returned to the United States. They established a residence in Key West, Florida. Hemingway's aim was to fit in among the fishermen and sailors who lived there. Their son Patrick was born in the summer of 1928 (his third son, Gregory, would be born three years later). Less than six months after Patrick's birth, Hemingway received a shock. His father, who had been worried about money and failing health, had shot and killed himself.

Many writers experience a "sophomore slump." After an outstanding first book, their second book is not as successful. That wasn't the case with Hemingway. His next novel, *A Farewell to Arms,* was published in 1929. The critics and the general public gave it the same reception as *The Sun Also Rises.* The novel drew from his personal experience of a decade earlier, when he had been wounded and fallen in love with Agnes.

By this time, the short stories and the two novels had revealed the characteristics of what eventually became known as the Hemingway hero. He was a man of action who exhibited "grace under pressure," or keeping a cool head, in the face of extreme danger. He often faced this danger by himself. In addition, he always remained true to his personal code of honor.

In many cases, there is a clear distinction between writers and the characters they create. That isn't the case with Hemingway. Sometimes it can be difficult to find the dividing line between the facts of Hemingway's life and the fictional lives of his characters. He felt that he had to show the same bravery and courage as his heroes. Sometimes he did. Sometimes he let people believe he did.

Around him, the United States was just entering the Great Depression. The quality of life for millions of Hemingway's countrymen was eroding. Hemingway would have none of that. He was about to become larger than life.

FYInfo

Bullfighting

The national sport of Spain, bullfighting dates back to Greek and Roman times when bulls were sacrificed to the gods. The modern sport took shape in the eighteenth century and has evolved into a precise ritual.

The *corrida*, as bullfights are known in Spanish, begins with a procession around the arena. The *corrida* has six individual contests, with three matadors taking turns. The bulls they face are specially bred for the bullring, and weigh well over 1,000 pounds.

Each fight, which normally lasts for about twenty minutes, begins with the release of the bull into the ring. Several footmen circle the animal as they wave large capes. The matador watches carefully to determine how the bull reacts. Then the first phase gets under way. Several picadors, men mounted on blindfolded horses that are covered by heavy protective pads, provoke the bull into attacking. The picadors stab the bull with long lances to weaken its neck muscles, which makes it difficult for the bull to hold up its head.

In the second phase, several banderilleros cautiously circle the bull, then stab the bull's neck with long darts wrapped in colorful ribbons. This action makes it more difficult for the animal to turn its head.

A Matador and Bull

Then comes the most famous—and dangerous—part. The matador uses his red cape to urge the bull to repeatedly pass within a few inches of his body. The crowd often shouts "Olé!" after each pass. When the matador senses that the bull has become sufficiently weakened, he moves directly in front. He leans in over the bull's horns and thrusts his sword into its neck, hoping to penetrate all the way to the heart. The bull collapses and dies.

If the crowd feels the matador has performed well, it will wave white handkerchiefs. The presiding judge may award the matador the bull's ears and tail. On rare occasions, the matador is unable to kill the bull. When that happens, the bull returns to the farm where it was raised and, after healing, enjoys a peaceful retirement.

Hemingway enjoyed being outdoors. He traveled to Africa to hunt big game in 1932. Here he poses with three animals that he shot during his safari.

Chapter 4

CREATING THE LEGEND

Hemingway had never liked his first name. From the time he was young, he had used a variety of nicknames. Now he adopted the one by which he would become known for the rest of his life: Papa Hemingway.

Even though he was barely in his thirties and had been famous for only a few years, as "Papa" he began acting as if he were one of the most important writers of his era. He had already "repaid" Sherwood Anderson for his assistance by writing a cruel parody of Anderson's work called *The Torrents of Spring.* Then he tried to tell Fitzgerald how to write. He publicly insulted several other people who had helped him. In turn, he was attacked in print for some of his attitudes. He responded by threatening to beat up the editors who had allowed those attacks to be published.

In 1932 he published *Death in the Afternoon.* A book about bullfighting, it met with mixed reviews. That same year he went to Africa for a safari. It was another way of testing his manhood. He shot a number of animals, including a lion.

Two years later, he bought a boat, which he named *Pilar* after a secret nickname that Pauline had used when Hemingway had first met her. He developed a reputation as an outdoor sportsman. His fame began to spread beyond his writing. He was becoming a celebrity.

"Great fisherman, great writer," biographer Anthony Burgess explains. "Ernest became one of the tourist attractions of Key West, drinking in dungarees in Sloppy Joe's [a famous bar where people still go to honor Hemingway], a man's man, an amiable bully, fit, brown, muscular, ready to fight gloved or barefisted."[1]

The Spanish Civil War broke out in 1936. Against Pauline's objections, Ernest accepted an offer to serve as a war correspondent. Just before leaving, he met a woman in Sloppy Joe's named Martha Gellhorn. Highly intelligent, she was a writer herself, and there was an immediate attraction between them. He followed her on the train to Miami and then to New York. Then he went off to cover the war. Gellhorn, who had also been hired to report on the fighting, soon arrived. When they weren't writing about battles, Hemingway and Gellhorn spent a lot of time with each other.

Hemingway made a trip to Paris to meet Pauline, who was trying to save the marriage. It didn't work.

When Ernest returned to the United States, he began to write a novel based on what he had seen in Spain. *For Whom the Bell Tolls* was published in 1940. It was a Book-of-the-Month Club selection, which guaranteed huge sales. It also revived his reputation, which had begun to suffer because he hadn't written anything notable for more than a decade.

By this point his marriage to Pauline had fallen apart. Late that year he married Martha. It didn't take long for cracks to appear, in this marriage, either. Both Hadley and Pauline had devoted themselves to him. Martha was different. She was an ambitious writer herself and often put her own interests ahead of his. That attitude was hard for Hemingway to accept.

World War II had broken out in 1939 with the German invasion of Poland. The United States became involved in the fighting when the Japanese attacked Pearl Harbor, Hawaii, on December 7, 1941. Hemingway wasn't content to be a mere bystander. In his forties, he was too old for official military service, but he still wanted to be involved. He fitted out *Pilar* as a sort of anti-submarine boat. The idea was that he and his crew would pretend to be a harmless fishing party. They would approach German U-boats that had surfaced to charge their batteries. When they got close enough, they would open up with concealed guns and try to throw grenades down the submarine's conning tower. When months went by without seeing any enemies, Hemingway wanted to do something else. In 1944, he went to Europe as a war correspondent. Martha accompanied him, but the problems in their relationship were obvious. They took verbal potshots at each other, often in public.

Hemingway wasn't content to just chronicle the action. He wanted to become directly involved. This was illegal because he wasn't supposed to be armed, but he ignored the law. It would be another opportunity for him to prove his bravery.

He often carried a rifle. One time he threw grenades into a cellar. For a while he even acted as if he were a commanding officer. "He sent French partisans [resistance fighters] out on regular patrols," reports Richard B. Lyttle. "He integrated a detachment from the Fifth Infantry Division into his little corps. He persuaded division supply officers to send up arms and ammunition for his Frenchmen. He set up a command post and arsenal."[2]

His fourth marriage was about to begin. True to form, the relationship began while he was still married to someone else. His new flame, Mary Welsh, was a writer for *Time* magazine. From the moment they met at a restaurant, they were attracted to each other. Welsh had the main qualities that Hemingway wanted in a woman: She flattered him and took care of him.

Although Hemingway's marriage to Martha would easily dissolve, Mary's husband made it difficult for Mary to divorce. Ernest was very unhappy about that. He was used to getting his way. One time, in a fit of drunken rage, he shot up a restroom.

The war ended in 1945 and so did his marriage to Martha. Even though it was his shortest, it had a long-lasting legacy. Martha had discovered a small farm in Cuba called La Finca Vigia (The Lookout Farm). It was a wonderful place to live, with beautiful gardens, a tennis court and swimming pool, and lots of cats.

Finally Mary got a divorce, and she and Ernest could marry. The newlyweds settled in La Finca Vigia in 1946.

Hemingway was too restless to stay in one place for very long. He and Mary made a long trip to Europe in 1947. In Venice, Italy, Hemingway met a young woman named Adriana Ivancich. Unlike his other relationships with women, this one remained on the level of friendship.

Adriana's friendship at this point in his career was especially valuable. Hemingway was going through another dry spell in his writing. Adriana helped to inspire him. She served as the model for one of the main characters in *Across the River and Into the Trees,* which was about an American military officer in his fifties and a young woman from Venice. Hemingway thought it was his best novel. Critics thought the opposite. They gave it a chilly reception. Some of them even said that he was washed up as a writer. Hemingway may have been discouraged, but he kept working. Soon his perseverance would pay off.

FYInfo

F. Scott Fitzgerald

Born in St. Paul, Minnesota in 1896, Francis Scott Key Fitzgerald was a relative of the man who wrote "The Star-Spangled Banner." Fitzgerald's first published writing was a detective story that appeared in his school paper when he was thirteen.

As a student at Princeton University, Fitzgerald became very involved in literary activities. He left Princeton before graduating and in 1917 was commissioned as a second lieutenant in the U.S. Army. Believing that he would die in World War I, he wrote a novel and sent it to Charles Scribner's Sons, a New York publisher. It was rejected.

In 1918, he was assigned to a military installation in Alabama. There he met Zelda Sayre, a beautiful young woman who had many suitors. Scott and Zelda became engaged. The war ended before Fitzgerald could go overseas. He went to New York and took a low-paying job with an advertising agency. Tired of waiting for him to make enough money to marry, Zelda broke off the engagement.

Soon he quit his New York job and went back to St. Paul to rewrite his novel. Scribner's accepted it. Entitled *This Side of Paradise,* it brought him instant fame when it was published in 1920. He married Zelda soon afterward. Their daughter and only child, Frances Scott "Scottie" Fitzgerald, was born the following year.

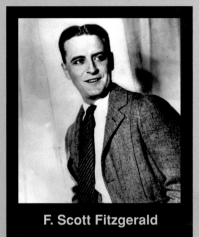

F. Scott Fitzgerald

In 1924, the family moved to France so that Fitzgerald could concentrate on his work. The following year he published *The Great Gatsby,* which most people consider to be his masterpiece. By then it was apparent that he and Zelda had serious marital problems. In 1930 she suffered a nervous breakdown and spent most of the rest of her life in mental institutions or undergoing psychiatric treatment. Fitzgerald had his own problems. He was an alcoholic.

Fitzgerald moved to Hollywood in 1937 and wrote several screenplays, though he only received credit for one. He began his final novel, *The Last Tycoon,* in 1939 but died the following year of a heart attack.

Fitzgerald believed himself to be a failure. His novels did not sell very well during his lifetime, but his reputation was revived after his death. He is regarded today as one of the most important twentieth-century American novelists.

Hemingway radiates good health as he stands on a hill overlooking a small Cuban fishing village. This village is very similar to the one he describes in "The Old Man and the Sea." Many people consider the book to be his finest work.

Chapter 5

THE FINAL TRIUMPH

For several years, Hemingway had been working on a long novel about the sea. Then he got an idea. He would publish one section of it separately.

It proved to be a good decision. The section was *The Old Man and the Sea.* As biographer Anthony Burgess notes, "Its impact was incredible. Sermons were preached on it, the author received a hundred laudatory letters every day, people kissed him, weeping, in the streets."[1]

A triumphant Hemingway set off for another African safari late in 1953. By this time, however, he was beginning to show signs of mental instability. It didn't help his condition that he was also drinking heavily. He shaved his head, trying to look like an African warrior. One day he went hunting with a spear. Fortunately, neither Hemingway nor any animals were injured.

Much worse was in store. On January 21, 1954, the Hemingways took off on a routine sightseeing flight from Nairobi, Kenya. They were over a spectacular waterfall when a flock of birds veered into the path of the aircraft. The plane crashed in the jungle.

Hemingway and his wife emerged with just a few scratches. They were quickly rescued and taken to the nearest airfield to go back to Nairobi. The airplane they boarded was barely airborne when it crashed and began to burn. Again Hemingway escaped, but he suffered several severe injuries.

At the end of the year, Hemingway was awarded the Nobel Prize for Literature. He claimed not to be impressed, saying that hardly anyone wrote anything that was of much value after receiving the award. He also didn't like the way that the citation was worded. The award was primarily for *The Old Man and the Sea,* and the citation suggested that some of his earlier books were not very good. Most Nobel laureates, as the prizewinners are called, are delighted to make the trip to Sweden to receive their awards and make a public speech. Not Hemingway. He said that he was still recovering from his injuries and couldn't go. Instead, the Swedish ambassador to Cuba presented him with the award.

Two years later Hemingway traveled to Spain. Everywhere he went he was honored and applauded. He spent a lot of time at bullfights, where matadors would often dedicate bulls to him. The trip had an additional benefit. Someone gave him two trunks that he had thought he had lost in 1928. They were filled with notes he had made while he was living in Paris. Hemingway was thrilled to recover them, and he used them to write a book that would be published after his death as *A Moveable Feast.*

He made yet another trip to Spain in 1959. The highlight was a twenty-four-hour party that Mary had organized to celebrate his sixtieth birthday. It included expensive imported food, fireworks, a shooting gallery, and friends who had flown in from many parts of the world. Several of them flew home convinced that Hemingway was seriously disturbed. Even Mary was unhappy. She threatened to leave him.

Meanwhile, at home in Cuba, a young man named Fidel Castro was leading an armed rebellion against the government. At

Fidel Castro led a revolt that overturned the government of Cuba in 1959. At first Castro was supported by the United States. That changed when he said he was a communist. Soon afterward, the discovery of Soviet missiles in Cuba theatened a nuclear war.

one point Hemingway was personally affected. An army patrol passed through La Finca Vigia and shot one of his dogs. Unsure how much longer he and Mary could stay there, he bought a home in Ketchum, Idaho.

His health was declining rapidly, and he was losing his mental faculties. He believed that people were after him, especially the

"Feds," or agents of the federal government. They weren't, but he wasn't convinced. His friends were becoming more and more concerned.

Hemingway still had a lot of energy. *Life* magazine asked him to do a long article about bullfighting. They asked for 10,000 words. He wrote 120,000. The magazine cut the article nearly in half and ran it in three consecutive issues. Entitled *Dangerous Summer,* the articles would be published in book form in 1985.

His decline continued. His fights with Mary became more intense. One time they threatened each other with guns—but she still cared deeply for him. When he talked about committing suicide, she convinced him to undergo electric shock treatments at the famous Mayo Clinic in Rochester, Minnesota. The treatments didn't help much, and he went back home to Ketchum. One spring morning Mary and his doctor talked him out of using a shotgun on himself. Then he tried to walk into the spinning propeller of an airplane that was preparing to take off.

Hemingway went back to the clinic. Eventually the doctor thought he could be discharged. He returned home.

On the morning of July 2, 1961, Hemingway woke up early. He found the key that unlocked his gun cabinet. He took out a double-barreled shotgun, loaded it, and put the barrels to his forehead. He pulled the trigger.

Ernest Hemingway was dead.

Generally when a writer dies, so does his publishing career. Occasionally a book left unfinished at the time of death will be published later. In rare cases, two. It is a measure of Hemingway's reputation that no fewer than five books of his unfinished manuscripts eventually found their way into print: *A Moveable Feast* (1964), *Islands in the Stream* (1970), *The Dangerous Summer* (1985), *The Garden of Eden* (1986), and *True at First Light* (published on July 21, 1999, to coincide with the 100th anniversary of his birth).

Another measure of his reputation is the Ernest Hemingway Foundation, which his widow Mary founded in 1965. It conducts a weeklong conference every other year, publishes the *Hemingway Review* and *Hemingway Newsletter,* and provides funding for the Hemingway Foundation/PEN Award, a cash prize awarded annually to the author of the most outstanding first book of fiction published that year.

He is perhaps the most recognizable American writer of the twentieth century. As biographer Michael Reynolds asks, "What other American author has five of his houses preserved in three states [Illinois, Florida, and Idaho] and one foreign country [Cuba]? What other author has a street named for him in Pamplona, a line of sporting goods in New York, a look-alike contest in Key West, a fishing contest in Havana, an annual PEN literary award, and a bad-writing contest in Venice?"[2]

An issue of *Time* magazine published near the end of the twentieth century featured 100 of the most important artists and entertainers of the 1900s. Six of them were writers. The photos of five of them—T. S. Eliot, Ralph Ellison, James Joyce, Franz Kafka, and Virginia Woolf—wouldn't have been recognized by most people without the captions that identified them. Even though Hemingway's picture also had an identifying caption, it really didn't need it.

By then he had become so famous that he was almost instantly recognizable. His books, his lifestyle that emphasized physical fitness and being outdoors, his reputation for hard work—and his faults—created an image that we normally associate with movie stars. He was truly larger than life.

Every year, countless numbers of young readers experience Hemingway's works for the first time, and many of them continue to read them into adulthood. Nearly all of his books are still in print, and they continue to enjoy steady sales. There is no doubt that Hemingway is a classic American storyteller.

FYInfo

Fidel Castro and the Cuban Revolution

General Fulgencio Batista

In 1952, General Fulgencio Batista overthrew the government of Cuba and became the country's ruler. A young man named Fidel Castro opposed Batista. The following year he took part in an attack on a Cuban army barracks. It failed. Most of the attackers were killed. Castro was captured, then sent into exile. He returned, and from his hiding place in the Sierra Maestra organized a revolt against Batista. Even though he and his men were badly outnumbered, he was usually able to inflict heavy casualties. Batista decided that he had had enough. Taking millions of dollars with him, he fled to Spain early in 1959. Castro and his followers—notably his brother Raul and Che Guevara—took over control of the government.

At first, the U.S. government supported Castro, but that support ended when the Cuban government took over some American businesses. It became apparent that the new regime was becoming allied with the Soviet Union. One of John F. Kennedy's first acts after becoming president was to supply a group of Cuban exiles who believed that the people would rise up against Castro if they went back to Cuba. They were wrong. Their invasion at the Bay of Pigs in April 1961 was a disaster. Nearly all the invaders were killed or captured when Kennedy refused to allow U.S. forces to become involved.

The Soviets secretly began to install nuclear missiles in Cuba. When American spy planes discovered the missiles in October 1962, Kennedy demanded their removal. The Soviets refused. The world was nearly plunged into a nuclear holocaust. After almost two tense weeks, the Soviets backed down.

Even though the United States still will not allow trade with Cuba (and it is very difficult for American citizens to travel there), Castro remains in power today. While many of the Cuban people remain in poverty, nearly all of them are able to read and write. The country has become famous for its athletes, particularly in baseball, boxing, and track and field.

CHRONOLOGY

1899 Born in Oak Park, Illinois, on July 21

1902 Catches first fish

1913 Begins high school

1917 Graduates from high school; takes job at *Kansas City Star*

1918 Goes to Italy as Red Cross ambulance driver and is seriously wounded

1921 Marries Hadley Richardson; moves to Paris

1923 Son John Hadley Nicanor is born

1926 Publishes *The Sun Also Rises*

1927 Marries Pauline Pfeiffer

1928 Son Patrick is born; father commits suicide

1929 Publishes *A Farewell to Arms*

1931 Son Gregory is born

1937 Goes to Spain as war correspondent

1940 Marries Martha Gellhorn

1944 Goes to Europe as a war correspondent

1946 Marries Mary Welsh

1953 Wins Pulitzer Prize for *Old Man and the Sea*

1954 Is awarded the Nobel Prize for Literature

1960 Moves to Ketchum, Idaho

1961 Commits suicide on July 2

1976 Mary Hemingway founds the Hemingway Foundation/PEN Award in honor of her late husband to recognize outstanding first novels

SELECTED WORKS

1923 *Three Stories & Ten Poems*

1924 *In Our Time*

1926 *The Sun Also Rises*

1929 *A Farewell to Arms*

1932 *Death in the Afternoon*

1940 *For Whom the Bell Tolls*

1950 *Across the River and Into the Trees*

1952 *The Old Man and the Sea*

1964 *A Moveable Feast*

1970 *Islands in the Stream*

1985 *The Dangerous Summer* (in book form)

1986 *The Garden of Eden*

1987 *The Complete Short Stories of Ernest Hemingway*

1999 *True at First Light*

FURTHER READING

For Young Adults

McDaniel, Melissa. *Ernest Hemingway*. Philadelphia: Chelsea House, 1996.

McDowell, Nicholas. *Hemingway*. Vero Beach, Florida: Rourke Enterprises, 1989.

Pratt, Paula Bryant. *The Importance of Ernest Hemingway*. San Diego, California: Greenhaven Press, 1998.

Whelan, Gloria. *The Pathless Woods: Ernest Hemingway's Sixteenth Summer in Northern Michigan*. Lansing, Michigan: Thunder Bay Press, 1998.

Yannuzzi, Della A. *Ernest Hemingway: Writer and Adventurer*. Springfield, New Jersey: Enslow Publishers, 1998.

Works Consulted

Baker, Carlos. *Hemingway: The Writer as Artist*. Princeton, New Jersey: Princeton University Press, 1990.

Burgess, Anthony. *Ernest Hemingway and His World*. New York: Charles Scribner's Sons, 1978.

Hemingway, Ernest. "The Big Two-Hearted River," in *In Our Time*. New York: Charles Scribner's Sons, 1925.

Hemingway, Ernest. *The Old Man and the Sea*. New York: Scribner Paperback Fiction, 1995.

Lyttle, Richard B. *Ernest Hemingway: The Life and the Legend*. New York: Atheneum, 1992.

Meyers, Jeffrey. *Hemingway: A Biography*. New York: Harper & Row, 1985.

Reynolds, Michael. *Hemingway: The Final Years*. New York: W.W. Norton, 1999.

Reynolds, Michael. *The Young Hemingway*. New York: W.W. Norton, 1998.

Voss, Frederick. *Picturing Hemingway: A Writer in His Time*. Washington, D.C.: Smithsonian Institution Press, 1999.

On the Internet

The Ernest Hemingway Foundation at Oak Park
http://ehfop.org/index.html

The Hemingway Resource Center
http://www.lostgeneration.com/

The Hemingway Society
http://www.hemingwaysociety.org/

Hemingway: A Retrospective
http://www.cnn.com/SPECIALS/books/1999/hemingway/index.html

FURTHER READING (CONT'D)

The Nobel Prize in Literature 1954
   http://nobelprize.org/literature/laureates/1954/
The Nobel Prize in Literature—Laureates
   http://nobelprize.org/literature/laureates/
A Brief Life of Fitzgerald
   http://www.sc.edu/fitzgerald/biography.html
"Information About Bullfighting in Spain and Andalucia"
   http://www.andalucia.com/bullfight/guide.htm
Cuban Revolution
   http://library.thinkquest.org/20176/crevolution.htm
Trask, David. "The Spanish-American War."
   http://www.loc.gov/rr/hispanic/1898/trask.html

GLOSSARY

amiable
(AY-mee-uh-bul)
easy to get along with.

callous
(KAH-lus)
without emotion; hardened; not feeling any sympathy for other people.

cynical
(SIH-nih-kull)
overly critical; believing that people are motivated only by selfish reasons.

dungarees
(dun-guh-REEZ)
pants made from coarse blue denim.

furled
(FURLD)
rolled tightly around a mast.

gored
(GORD)
pierced with a sharp object, such as a horn.

parody
(PAIR-uh-dee)
close imitation of an artistic work, usually for humorous effect.

INDEX

Anderson, Sherwood 24, 25, 26, 31
Batista, Fulgencio 42
Brodsky, Joseph 13
Buck, Pearl 13
Castro, Fidel 38, 42
Castro, Raul 42
Dewey, Admiral George 21
Eliot, T. S. 41
Ellison, Ralph 41
Faulkner, William 13
Fitzgerald, F. Scott 26, 31, 35
Fitzgerald, Scottie 35
Fitzgerald, Zelda Sayre 35
Guevara, Che 42
Gutiérrez, Carlos 10
Hancock, Tyley (uncle) 17
Hemingway, Carol (sister) 15
Hemingway, Clarence (father) ... 15, 17, 18, 27
Hemingway, Ernest
    Accident-prone 17
    Becomes "Papa Hemingway" 31
    Birth of 15
    Bullfighting and 25-26
    Buys home in Idaho 39
    Buys La Finca Vigia 34
    Death of 40
    Develops public image 31-32
    High school years 17-18
    Influenced by war stories 16-17
    Lives in Paris 24-27
    Love of fishing 7, 16
    Marries Hadley Richardson 24
    Marries Martha Gellhorn 32
    Marries Mary Welsh 34
    Marries Pauline Pfeiffer 27
    Moves to Key West 27
    Publishes The Sun Also Rises 26
    Serves as war correspondent ... 32, 33-34
    Suffers serious wound 23
    Volunteers for Red Cross 18-20
    Wins Nobel Prize 11-12, 38
    Works for *Kansas City Star* 18
    Works of
        Across the River and Into the Trees 34
        "The Big Two-Hearted River"
        .... 7-10, 26
        Dangerous Summer 40

Death in the Afternoon 31
A Farewell to Arms 27
For Whom the Bell Tolls 32
Garden of Eden 40
In Our Time 26
Islands in the Stream 40
A Moveable Feast 38
"My First Sea Voyage" 17
The Old Man and the Sea ....
.... 7, 10-12, 37, 38
The Sun Also Rises 26-27
Three Stories & Ten Poems 25
Torrents of Spring 31
True at First Light 40
Hemingway, Grace Hall (mother) ....
.... 15, 16, 17, 24, 27
Hemingway, Gregory (son) 27
Hemingway, Hadley (first wife) 24, 25, 27, 32
Hemingway, John Hadley Nicanor (son) ......
.... 26
Hemingway, Leicester (brother) 16
Hemingway, Madeleine ("Sunny," sister) ......
.... 15, 16
Hemingway, Marcelline (sister) 15, 16
Hemingway, Martha (third wife) ... 32, 33, 34
Hemingway, Mary (fourth wife) ....
34, 37, 38, 39, 40, 41
Hemingway, Patrick (son) 27
Hemingway, Pauline (second wife) 27, 32
Hemingway, Ursula (sister) 15
Ivancich, Adriana 34
Jackson, General Stonewall 16
Joyce, James 41
Kafka, Franz 41
Kennedy, President John F. 42
Lewis, Sinclair 13
Morrison, Toni 13
O'Neill, Eugene 13
Österling, Anders 12
Perkins, Maxwell 26
Pound, Ezra 24, 25
Roosevelt, Theodore 21
Singer, Isaac Bashevis 13
Stein, Gertrude 24
Steinbeck, John 13
von Kurowsky, Agnes 23, 24, 27
Woolf, Virginia 41